FINNISH
PROVERBS

LAND OF THE FINNS

My eyes have filled with tears
For I have been seeking
That *old* Finland,
That old, rural land and time
The early immigrants left behind,
Yet which remained forever
In their hearts and minds
So that their children,
And even their children's children
Yearned for that remote and unknown
Land of the Finns.

Inkeri Väänänen-Jensen

Preceding page:
The "hannunvaakuna", a square with loops
at the corners, is an ancient good-luck sign
and a favorite Finnish decorative motif.

FINNISH PROVERBS

Translated by
Inkeri Väänänen-Jensen

Front cover photograph of Finland
State Forest, Finland, Minnesota,
©1990 by Joan Liffring-Zug.
Back cover photograph of Finland
State Forest, Finland, Minnesota,
©1990 by Joan Liffring-Zug.

Calligraphy & illustrations
by Esther Feske.

Penfield
BOOKS

For a list of all ethnic titles :
 Penfield Books
 215 Brown Street
 Iowa City, IA 52245
 1-800-728-9998
 www.penfieldbooks.com
 www.facebook.com/penfield.books

Finland has over 180,000 lakes, some 30,000 islands and almost 3,000 miles of coastline. There's no shortage of waterfront locations for summer cottages and saunas, both necessities to the Finns.

Sources used for proverbs:
Laukkanen, Kari and Pekka Hakamies, *Finnish Proverbs (Sananlaskut)*, Finnish Literature Society, Helsinki, Finland, 1984.
Lönnrot, Elias, *Proverbs of the Finnish People (Suomen kansan sananlaskuja)*, Weilin-Goos, Tampere, Finland, 1981. First published in 1842.

THE AUTHOR

A translator of Finnish literature, Inkeri Väänänen-Jensen is also a poet and essayist. Born to Finnish immigrant parents, she grew up in Virginia, Minnesota, and has degrees in English and Finnish from the University of Minnesota.

She has collaborated with others on a Helmi Mattson Reader. Mattson (1890-1974), a Finnish-American, served the immigrants as an editor, novelist, poet, essayist, and short story writer. This project is sponsored by the Immigration History Research Center of the University of Minnesota.

Inkeri served as co-editor of a book presenting Finnish-American and Finnish writers from the writing workshop at the 1987 Reunion of Sisters Conference in Kuopio, Finland. This book is sponsored by the Center for Finnish Studies, University of Minnesota. In 1982, Nordic Translators published *Finnish Short Stories*, compiled and translated by Inkeri. She has finished a manuscript, *Inkeri's Journey*, about her life as a Finnish immigrant child on Minnesota's Iron Range.

INTRODUCTION

Finland's rich sources of folk literature contain homey philosophy, pithy suggestions, earthy slices of advice, familiar truths, bits of wisdom, and sometimes just plain common sense.

There are more than a million Finnish proverbs and sayings in the archives of the Finnish Literature Society in Helsinki.

Finns say that proverbs contribute in three ways to their national solidarity. First, proverbs preserve much of their forebears' knowledge, customs, and counsel. Second, they beautify and strengthen the speech of the nation; they add to the pungency of human discourse. Third, their proverbs serve as guides to those who wish to study Finnish language and life.

Enjoy these short, pithy statements from the land where the *Kalevala**was born, where words, not swords, were the tools of the magicians.

Inkeri Väänänen-Jensen

*epic poem of the Finns, based on the songs of the folk.

THE FINNISH SPIRIT

Laughter prolongs life.

NAURU PIDENTÄÄ IKÄÄ.

One of the most imposing of Finland's Medieval castles, Olavinlinna (Olaf's Castle) houses the Savonlinna Opera Festival every July.

Let us sing the old songs
    when the new ones
        have all been sung.

Advice is good;
        help is better.

Know your own worth;
        recognize another's.

It is good to live in hope.

A Finn does not
        believe something
            until he tests it.

None is so short
        he needn't stoop and
            none is so tall
                he needn't reach.

The mind is precious,
        for you always need it.

Music festivals of all kinds are held through-
out Finland each summer. Like this folk music
festival, they draw thousands of visitors,
Finns and tourists alike.

Peasants & clumps of willows
    are hard to destroy.

Not all sleep
        who are lying down.

Do not make a coat out of
          birchbark.

We live as we can,
      not as we may wish.

It is sad
    to dance in another's shoes.

Even a little bargain
        is a bargain.

A birchbark sheath and
    a leather button
      cost nothing.

The kantele, ancient musical instrument of Finland, is thought to date back more than 2000 years. It makes a light, tinkling sound when played and is related to the zither.

If you don't get what you want
and don't want
what you can get,
then you will do without.

Who promises much
gives little.

Happiness shared
is twice enjoyed.

A sharp blade
is the glory of a knife,
the mind the glory of a man.

Speak only the truth,
even if it means
only one word a day.

LOVE & THE FAMILY

Love does not rust.

EI RAKKAUS RUASTU.

Rya (ryijy) rugs, popular in mid-18th to early
19th centuries, have enjoyed a 20th-century

When the copperware shines,
the kitchen is beautiful.

When thinking of yourself,
you have no time
for others.

Poverty and love
are impossible to hide.

Tell me who your friends are,
and I will tell you
what you are.

You are rich if you have love.

revival. These thick tufted weavings, substitutes for animal furs, can be used on floors, walls, or as bed coverings.

CHILDREN

N̲o one is a master at birth.

EI KUKAAN OLE MESTARI SYNTYISÄS.

Artisans blow and shape molten glass into a bowl. Finland is famous for its handmade crafts and for products designed to retain handmade qualities while being mass-produced. Finnish glass, ceramics, cutlery, toys, textiles and furniture are enjoyed worldwide. 12

The child who is always led
will never walk alone.

The child does away from home
what he sees done at home.

Even the king's son is a child.

No child is so bad that
he's not welcome at home.

Sleep is medicine to a child.

The floor
serves as the child's chair.

There is no child
who does not cry
and no cloth
that cannot be cut.

A BETTER WAY

B etter once too much
than always too little.

PAREMPI KERRAN LIIKA

KUIN AINA NIUKKA.

Traditional birch-bark and split-wood baskets
assume many sizes and shapes for endless
uses. They reflect the Finns' restrained balance
between appearance and purpose of the object.

Better a good separation
than a poor union.

Better to look ahead than behind.

Better the bitter truth
than a sweet lie.

Better to give than to take.

Better one mark in the bank
than two in the pocket.

Better to laugh than to cry.

Better a good friend
than a poor relative.

Better two than one.

Better one load in the barn
than two outside.

Rural furniture of two or three centuries ago
may seem crude, but its frugality of design
and honesty of materials can still be found
in modern furniture from Finland. Contemporary industrial designers are known and
respected for maintaining aesthetic and
social values in the objects that shape
Finnish culture.

Better to drive than to push.

Better a small gift
   than a big promise.

Better a good end
   than a showy beginning.

Better a day early
      than two days late.

Better a small potato
      than an empty pot.

Following page:
Sauna accessories are simple and functional:
wood buckets and water dippers remain
touchable in the extreme heat; leafy birch
switches stimulate circulation; linen towels or
soft root brushes help cleanse the skin. The
steamy heat of the sauna is followed by a
quick dip in the lake or a roll in the snow. Finns
believe the repeated heatings and coolings have
physical, social and psychological benefits
and promote stamina.

WORDS OF WISDOM

If a sauna, whiskey and tar
do not help,
  the disease is fatal.

JOS EI SAUNA JA VIINA JA TERVA

AUTA NIIN SE TAUTI ON KUOLEMAKSI.

One who asks
         does not get lost.

It is difficult to grow old,
 but more difficult to be old.

Dying
     is the most difficult task,
     leaving home the saddest.

Do not rejoice
       over another's misfortune,
          for your turn will come.

One hour of thinking
       equals two hours of work.

Spilled water
          cannot be retrieved.

An accident does not advertise
          its coming.

The Finnish coat of arms is based on this
1591 coat of arms from King Gustavus Vasa's
tombstone in Uppsala Cathedral in Sweden.
For over seven centuries, Finland was ruled
by its neighbors, Sweden and Russia.

One castle
cannot hold two kings.

Think first and then speak.

None is so foolish there isn't
someone more foolish,
none so wise there isn't
someone wiser.

It is a poor bird that cannot
carry its own feathers.

Good news travels far,
bad news even farther.

A sword kills one,
but a tongue
kills thousands.

Do not lend your bicycle
or your wife to anyone.

A statue of Russian Czar Alexander II stands
in Helsinki's historic Senate Square. During
Alexander's reign, reforms benefitted Finnish
self-government and national identity.
Senate Square is surrounded by the Great
Cathedral of Evangelical Lutheranism, shown,
Helsinki University and Government
buildings, all in a unified neo-classical style.

Even the stupid seem wise
                if they do not speak.

Who is timid in a crowd
            is brave in the corner.

You cannot carry
            all the water from a lake.

Eyes
            are the mirror of the soul.

A good person
                values even himself.

He is truly a liar
                who believes his own lie.

You sing the song of the one
                who owns the sleigh.

This monument in Helsinki honors Baron
Carl Gustaf Emil Mannerheim, a 20th-
century hero. He was a World War I general
for the Czar, military leader and Regent for
Finland after independence from Russia in
1917, Field Marshal to repel the Soviet
invasions of 1939-40 and World War II, and
President 1944-46.

You can fool others only once,
but yourself for a lifetime.

We all know how
to live another's life,
if not our own.

What you do not repair,
you destroy.

The ear hears more
than the eye can see.

Who ignores the gift
ignores the giver.

An empty sack
cannot stand alone.

What has no beginning
has no end.

Made of steel tubes rising to about thirty feet, and a separate portrait sculpture, this monument in Helsinki honors Jean Sibelius, composer of universally loved music.

No fire is so hidden that
        its smoke cannot be seen.

A debt paid is forgotten.

A tree does not fall
        with one blow.

A fallen tree cannot rise.

Life passes one day at a time.

He is master who rules himself.

POVERTY & PLENTY

Bread is not buttered
on both sides.

EI MOLEMMILLE PUOLIN VOITA LEIVÄLLE.

Eliel Saarinen influenced 20th-century
architecture in both Finland and America.
His Helsinki Railway Station (1914), monumen-
tal and fanciful at the same time, is regarded
as a masterpiece. He moved to the United
States in 1922, became president of the
Cranbrook Academy of Art, and revolutionized
skyscraper construction.

Not every tree has a squirrel.

No one so rich he needs no help,
no one so poor
he cannot help.

Wealth may be hidden;
poverty always shows.

There's none so poor
that there's no inheritance.

Who is satisfied with little
remains poor.

He is poor who has no soul.

Poverty
comes first to the woodshed,
then to the barn, and
finally to the house.

*Finlandia Hall, a strikingly modern concert
and convention facility in Helsinki, was one
of the last works by internationally known
designer and architect Alvar Aalto. Behind it
are, left, the Parliament Building, and right,
the tower of the National Museum.*

When poverty
steps inside the door,
love flies out the window.

If nothing is dropped,
nothing will be found.

A full purse does not jingle.

The moon
is a poor man's lamp.

A rooster
is a poor man's clock.

A wife
is a poor man's hired hand.

Sauna—
the poor man's drugstore.

RELIGION & HOPE

Nothing is so deep
that it has no bottom.

EI NIIN SYVÄÄ ETTEI POHJAA LÖYÄ.

Built in the capital city of Helsinki in 1969,
Taivallahti Church is modern Finnish
architecture at its boldest. Cut into solid
granite, it is finished with wood, glass, a
copper dome, and Finnish textiles.

No day is so long
     that evening does not come.

No night is so long
     that day does not follow.

The day is longer
          in the morning.

He lives as if it is his last day.

Think each day
     that you may die
          but also that you may
               live to be a hundred.

No one dies twice.

There is time enough to rest
               in the grave.

This 15th-century church of St. Anne in
Kumlinge, in the eastern islands of Åland, is
one of about eighty graystone churches built
in Finland during the Middle Ages.

You do not reach heaven
                in one jump.

Repentance after death
                is too late.

When you seek good,
        you find something better.

A thousand begins with one.

God protects a man
                even on the sea.

The time for miracles is not over.

Most large things
                once were small.

Even God laughs when
        a thief steals from a thief.

NATURE & THE SEASONS

The forest gives
what the forest has.

METTÄ ANTAA, MITÄ METTÄL ON.

Lingon or cloudberries, cranberries and
mushrooms lure adults and children to the
woods.

A summer cottage
brings two happy days:
   first, when you finish it,
      and second, when
         you get it sold.

Two things are beautiful
      in summer:
   leaves on the trees
and grass on the ground.

When men haul out the timber,
   the fields grow flowers.

The man feeds the field,
      the field feeds the man.

During the summer
      one does not think of
            winter.

Log cabins, invented by the ancient Finns, are making a comeback as desirable country-style houses. Using the abundant forests to create shelter from the extremes of weather shows typical Finnish self-sufficiency.

During the summer
    you don't have time,
        and in winter it's too cold.

If only it were always
        summer and Sunday
        and never
            winter or Monday.

Who remembers
        the bitter cold of winter
        does not complain
            of summer's heat.

The north wind is always cold,
        no matter where
            it comes from.

The weather hinders even war.

The Lapps, inhabitants of the far north, traditionally herd reindeer, snare grouse, fish and pick berries. Reindeer are used to pull sleds and for meat, and Lapps still wear their colorful national costumes.

One cannot ski
    without leaving a trace.

When you hear
        the call of the loon,
            stay off the ice.

As spring nears, cares recede.

February's gentle winds
    are paid for in March.

Winter does not leave
        without looking back.

The sun is shining,
        rain is falling,
            summer must be coming.

Not even the sun shines
        until it rises.

Public access to nature is guaranteed by law and custom: anyone may walk in the woods, pick berries, and swim in the lakes, as long as they keep a proper distance from homes.

Not all clouds bring rain.

The road often used
never yields to grass.

The rabbit thinks he's hidden
when his head is in a bush.

A bird does not fly
until his wings
are ready to carry him.

The land will not give unless
the land receives.

FOOD & DRINK

A fish is beautiful in the water,
but more beautiful
in the pan.

KAUNIS ON KALA VEDESSÄ,

KAUNIHIMPI KATTILASSA.

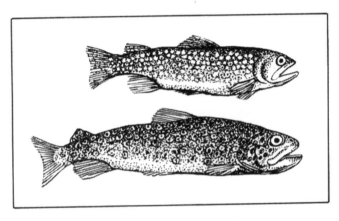

Fishing, boating, swimming, hiking, camping,
panning for gold, cross-country and downhill
skiing are outdoor activities available to all
Finns in the national parks.

The biggest fish
    is in another's boat.

Today's egg is better than
                tomorrow's chicken.

The crust is also bread.

It is still cake
            even if it is in crumbs.

You need skill
        even if you're peeling turnips.

Until the food is ready
        feed your guests with words.

PHILOSOPHY

Do not go barehanded
into a hawk's nest.

EI PIRÄ MENNA PALJAIN
KÄSIN HAUKAN PESÄLLE.

Begun in the 1280s, this castle in Turku is now
restored as a museum with banquet and
conference rooms for the city. The Turku Music
Festival is held on the grounds each August.
Turku, the old capital of Finland, is a thriving
shipping and university city.

Not all are fishermen
who are in the boat.

An ax is not sharpened
on only one side.

Even the most wise
makes one mistake.

You may close your own gate
but not another's mouth.

The new is not so good
that one forgets the old.

Every man can tell you how,
even if he can't do it.

Do not sell the bear's skin
until you've caught the bear.

If you don't go you can't return.

The Porvoo cathedral, with its decorative
brick gable, looms over riverfront storehouses
and homes painted red, yellow and white.
Like many Finnish cities, Porvoo is preserving
the sturdy and practical buildings from its
past.

A weak agreement is better than a strong quarrel.

Joy is the daughter of peace.

If you can't get through, walk around.

Your own pain teaches you to know another's pain.

The sea begins with a drop, savings with a penny.

Do not fly farther than your wings can carry you.

Keep learning as long as you live.

Hurry slowly.

"Kalevala Koru" (ornaments), reproductions of antique jewelry, provide contemporary wearers with a link to their past.

Made in the USA
Charleston, SC
17 June 2012